THE USBORNE BOOK OF
EASY
FLUTE
TUNES

Katie Elliott and Emma Danes

Designed by Linda Penny

Illustrated by Adrienne Kern
Photography by Howard Allman

Original music and arrangements by Katie Elliott
Series editor: Anthony Marks

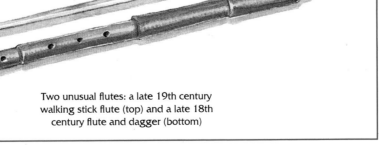

Two unusual flutes: a late 19th century
walking stick flute (top) and a late 18th
century flute and dagger (bottom)

Introduction

This is a book of tunes for you to play on your flute. As you go through it, new notes, musical words and signs are introduced. The tunes get more difficult later in the book, and you may need to spend longer practicing them. Near the end there are some tunes for two flutes, and some for flute and piano.

On page 46 there is a section called "Music help" which explains all the musical symbols used in the tunes. It reminds you what the Italian words mean, and tells you how to pronounce them. There is also a fingering chart. On page 47 there is a list of flute music you could try listening to and an index of the tunes in this book.

As well as tunes, this book also contains lots of information about playing and practising, flutes, composers and different musical styles.

First published in 1994 by Usborne Publishing Ltd, Usborne House, 83-85 Saffron Hill, London EC1N 8RT. First published in America, March 1995.

Copyright © 1994 Usborne Publishing Ltd. The name Usborne and the device 🎈 are Trade Marks of Usborne Publishing Ltd.

Printed in Portugal
AE

Your flute

People have played flutes in many parts of the world for thousands of years. Today they are used for all sorts of music, including folk, classical, jazz and pop. In the picture below you can see the names of all the different parts of your flute.

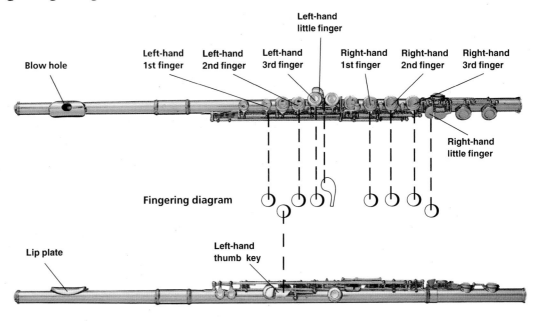

Lip plate

Blow hole

Rod

Body section

Head joint

Keys

Pin

Foot joint

Flutes have three sections, the head joint, body and foot joint. The head joint contains the blow hole. The keys are attached to the body and foot joint by metal rods and pins.

How to read the fingering diagrams in this book

On the right you can see which keys on your flute to press with each finger or thumb. Each time you learn a new note, there is a fingering diagram to show you which keys to press. In the diagram, there is a shape for each of the keys labelled in the picture. If the shape for a key is colored in, you have to press it down. If the shape is not colored in, you do not press the key down.

Blow hole

Left-hand 1st finger

Left-hand 2nd finger

Left-hand 3rd finger

Left-hand little finger

Right-hand 1st finger

Right-hand 2nd finger

Right-hand 3rd finger

Right-hand little finger

Fingering diagram

Lip plate

Left-hand thumb key

Putting your flute together

Hold the head joint and the body of the flute as shown above. Do not squeeze the keys.

Gently twist the parts together so that the blow hole is in line with the first key on the body.

Gently twist the foot joint into the body. Hold the body near the join with the head joint.

The rod on the foot joint should line up with the middle of the last key on the body.

How to hold your flute

Balance your flute on the side of your left-hand first finger and your right thumb, and curve your fingers over the keys. Do not grip the flute tightly.

WARNING!
Always handle your flute carefully. Banging it can stop the keys from fitting, and may leave a dent.

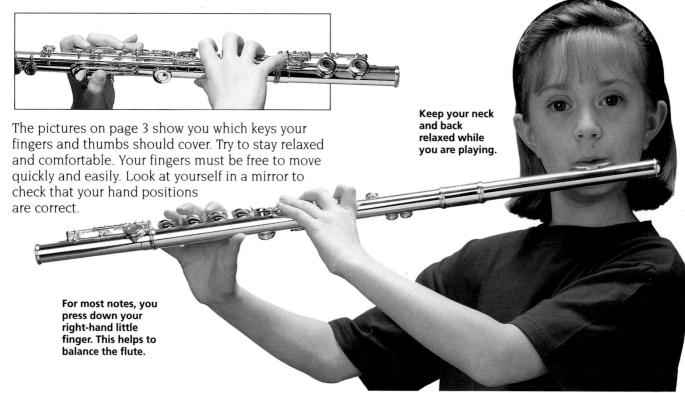

The pictures on page 3 show you which keys your fingers and thumbs should cover. Try to stay relaxed and comfortable. Your fingers must be free to move quickly and easily. Look at yourself in a mirror to check that your hand positions are correct.

Keep your neck and back relaxed while you are playing.

For most notes, you press down your right-hand little finger. This helps to balance the flute.

Making a sound

Press down the thumb and first three fingers of your left hand, and your right-hand little finger.

Put the flute just under your lower lip, covering a tiny bit of the blow hole. Looking in a mirror, position your lips so there is a small hole in the middle of them. This is so that you blow a strong stream of air, without any escaping at the sides. The shape of your lips is called your embouchure ("om-boo-shure").

Move your bottom jaw slightly forward to blow. Your face should look relaxed.

Try blowing until you can make a clear sound. This will get easier the more you practice.

Bring the flute up to your lips. Never bend down to it.

When you can make a sound, try starting each blow with a gentle "ta" sound. This will make the start of the note sound clearer.

Don't puff your cheeks out.

☒

Don't tighten your muscles as if you are smiling.

☒

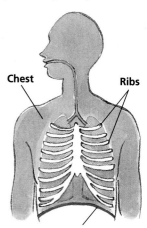

Your embouchure should look like this.

Breathing

When you play the flute, you have to take deep breaths using a muscle in your stomach called your diaphragm ("di-a-fram"). You can feel this muscle working when you cough or yawn.

Chest **Ribs**

Diaphragm

Practice using your diaphragm to help you breathe. To check you are doing this properly, put a hand just below your ribs and above your waist. As you take a breath push your stomach out, then pull it in as you breathe out. Keep your shoulders still. Can you feel how your diaphragm moves?

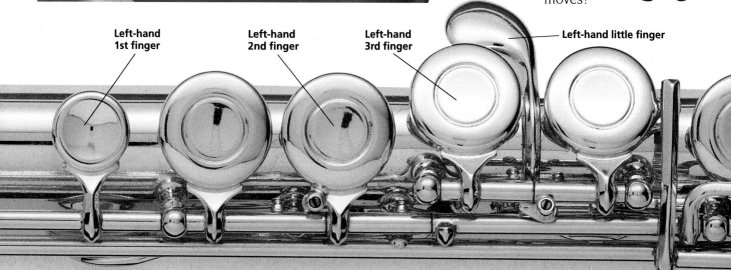

Left-hand 1st finger   **Left-hand 2nd finger**   **Left-hand 3rd finger**   **Left-hand little finger**

How to stand

It is best to play the flute standing up, so you can breathe easily. If you prefer to sit, make sure your back is straight and upright.

Keep your flute parallel to the floor.

This end should not droop down.

Prop your music up at eye level. Do not bend down to read it.

Use a music stand if you have one, so that you can adjust the height of your music.

Keep your feet slightly apart, and your weight evenly balanced.

Reading music

Music is written on a set of five lines called a staff (or stave). How high or low a note is is called its pitch. The higher the pitch, the higher up the staff it is. The pitch names go alphabetically from A to G, then start at A again. A sign called a treble clef means that a note on the second line up is G.

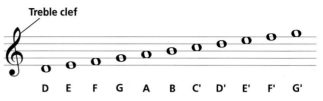

Treble clef

D   E   F   G   A   B   C'   D'   E'   F'   G'

The distance from one pitch to the next pitch up or down with the same letter name is called an octave. In this book, the pitch an octave above D is called D', the pitch an octave above E is E', and so on.

Counting

Note lengths are counted in beats. You can see the most common note lengths on the right:

Quarter note = 1 beat

Half note = 2 beats

Whole note = 4 beats o

Time signatures

Music is divided into sections called bars by vertical lines. At the start of a piece, a pair of numbers called a time signature tells you how to count. The top number tells you how many beats are in a bar. The bottom number tells you what kind of beats they are (4 means they are quarter notes).

This means 4 quarter beats in a bar.

This means 3 quarter beats in a bar.

Playing G

Here is a fingering diagram for G (the note you played on the last page), and G on a staff.

NEW NOTE   G

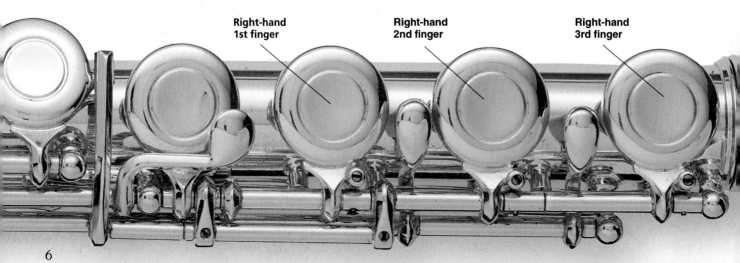

Right-hand 1st finger

Right-hand 2nd finger

Right-hand 3rd finger

Au clair de la lune

This is the tune to an old French song by Jean-Baptiste Lully (1632-1687). It is about two pantomime characters, Pierrot and Harlequin, talking in the moonlight.

NEW NOTE **A**

NEW NOTE **B**

German song

Remembering how to breathe

Each time you practice your flute, start with a few breathing exercises. Pretend to yawn to help you relax. Breathe using your diaphragm.

To check you are breathing correctly, try lying on the floor with a book on your diaphragm. The book should move up and down as you breathe.

The book should be just below your ribs.

Right-hand little finger

Playing C'

To play C', take your left thumb off its key. At first the flute might feel a bit off-balance, but it is safe resting on the side of your left-hand first finger and your right thumb. Your right-hand little finger helps to keep it stable too. Hold your flute like this for a while, to help you get used to balancing it.

J'ai du bon tabac

This is a French folk tune. Keep the rhythm very steady and even. Try to make each note last its full length, even if you feel a bit short of breath.

Air des bouffons

This tune was written to go with a type of French dance called bouffons or matachins. Bouffons was a very skillful sword dance, often performed in front of an audience. It was popular from the 16th century to the 18th century.

A 16th century drawing of bouffons

Dotted half notes

A dot after a note increases its length by half. A dotted half note lasts for a half note plus half a half note, or three quarter note beats.

Barcarolle

This tune is by Jacques Offenbach (1819-1880).
Offenbach was a very popular composer of comic
songs and operettas (light-hearted plays set to
music). This piece is from one of his best known
operettas, *The Tales of Hoffmann*.

Barcarolles are based on songs sung by boatmen in
Venice. They have a lilting rhythm and melody to
suggest a boat moving through water.

Boats in Venice

Oily rag

This tune is in an American style known as ragtime
which was popular from the late 19th century until
the 1920s. Ragtime tunes often have unusual
rhythms. A composer named Scott Joplin (1868-
1917) wrote many famous piano rags, including *The
Entertainer* and *Maple Leaf Rag*.

A band
playing
ragtime

Flats

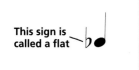

This sign is called a flat

A flat sign before a note makes its pitch slightly lower. In the next tune, the Bs have flat signs before them, making them B flats. A flat sign affects all the notes after it in the bar on the same line or space. A flat sign during a piece is called an accidental.

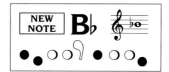

NEW NOTE **B♭**

Ode to joy

This tune is by a German composer, Ludwig van Beethoven (1770-1827). It comes from his last symphony, which he wrote when he was completely deaf. Today it is used as the national anthem of the European Community.

Beethoven

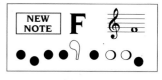

NEW NOTE **F**

Humming song

This tune is from a collection of 43 piano pieces by Robert Schumann (1810-1856). Schumann gave the first seven pieces to his eldest daughter as a birthday present. On the right is a picture of Leipzig in Germany, where Schumann lived for a while.

Making a good sound

Remember to keep your flute level as you play.

Do not grip too hard and keep your wrists relaxed.

Start your practice each day by playing some long, steady notes. Try altering the position of your flute and embouchure slightly so you can find how to make the best sound.

Try starting some long notes quietly and making them get gradually louder. Blow a bit harder to make the note get louder. Remember to take deep breaths and let the air out gradually so the notes sound even.

Rests

Quarter rest	𝄽
Half rest	▬
Whole rest	▬

Silences in music are called rests. You count them just like notes. A quarter rest lasts for one quarter beat, a half rest for two quarter beats and a whole rest for four quarter beats. A whole rest is also used to show a rest lasting a full bar.

Roses from the south

This tune is a waltz by Johann Strauss II (1825-1899). A waltz is a type of dance which became popular at the end of the 18th century. It has three beats in a bar. Strauss wrote many famous dance tunes, including By the Beautiful Blue Danube.

Dancing a waltz

Hints to help you practice

✔ Practice regularly and often. You will learn more easily if you practice for five or ten minutes several times a day than if you play for an hour once a week.

✔ Start with long notes to practice breathing and sound control.

✔ Use a mirror to check the position of your lips and hands.

✔ Stand up straight so you can breathe easily.

✔ Practice any difficult bars in the music separately until you can play them well.

✔ To avoid making mistakes, learn tunes slowly at first.

✔ When you know some tunes well, give a short concert for your friends.

Tonguing

When you play a tune, you can make each note sound clear by starting it with a "ta" sound. This is called tonguing. Try tonguing a note gently several times. (Do not tongue too fiercely, or it will sound breathy and uncontrolled.) Then try tonguing several different notes, making sure you move your fingers and tongue at exactly the same time.

Keep your lips and bottom jaw still as you say "ta".

Slurs

Slurs are curved lines joining notes of different pitches. They tell you to play smoothly. Tongue only the first note in a slur, then keep playing without tonguing until the last slurred note.

Oats, peas, beans

Loud and quiet

p	This stands for *piano*
f	This stands for *forte*

The signs on the left are called dynamics. They tell you how loudly to play. *Piano* means "quiet" and *forte* means "loud".

Breath marks

,	Good place to breathe
(,)	Possible place to breathe

These marks show you where to take a breath without interrupting the music. Try not to take a breath anywhere else.

Little John

Eighth note

An eighth note lasts for half a quarter note. Eighth notes can be linked in groups.

Eighth note ♪

Pair of eighth notes

Repeats

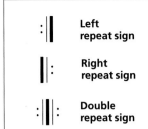

	Left repeat sign
	Right repeat sign
	Double repeat sign

A repeat sign with dots on the left tells you to play the last section of music again. You go back to the last repeat sign with dots on the right, or if there are no earlier repeat marks, you go back to the beginning of the piece. When you reach the same repeat sign for the second time, ignore it and finish the piece. When you see a repeat sign with dots on the left and the right, repeat the section before it and the section after it.

Tempo di minuetto

This tune is by a composer named James Hook (1746-1827). It is in the style of an elegant French dance called a minuet (shown on the right). Repeat the first section, then play the second section and repeat that too.

NEW NOTE **E**

Looking after your flute

Always clean your flute when you finish your practice for the day. This will keep it shiny and in good condition. The pictures below show you what to do.

Clean the lip plate with a damp cloth and then polish it with a dry one.

Thread a thin cloth through a cleaning rod and loop it over so the rod is not showing. Dry the inside of all three parts of the flute.

Dry the pads under the keys by pressing each key down onto a small piece of very thin paper.

Gently wipe the whole flute (avoiding the rods and pins) with a soft, dry cloth.

Then carefully put it away in its case. Make sure all the keys are facing upward so they don't get damaged.

More dotted notes   Ties

A dot after a quarter note makes it last for one and a half quarter beats. 𝅘𝅥.

Two notes tied together

A tie is a curved line linking two notes of the same pitch. Tongue the first note, then do not breathe or tongue again until you reach the end of the tie. This means that instead of playing two separate notes you play one long note lasting the length of both the tied notes added together.

Round-O

A Round-O (called *rondeau* in French, or *rondo* in Italian) is a piece made up of short sections, a bit like a song with different verses and a repeated chorus. The music keeps coming back to the chorus, as though it is going around in a circle. See if you can spot the chorus and verses in this tune, and watch out for the tied notes too. *Moderato* means "at a moderate speed", not too fast or too slow.

A medieval French composer, Baude Cordier, wrote out this rondeau in a circle shape.

Sharps

A sharp sign in front of a note makes its pitch slightly higher. It also affects all the notes after it in the bar on the same line or space.

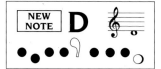

Aiken drum

The Prince of Denmark's march

This tune is by an English composer, Jeremiah Clarke (1674-1707). It was written for keyboard, but today it is usually played on the trumpet, often on special occasions. Marches have two or four beats in a bar.

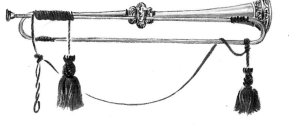

Playing low notes

Low notes, such as D and E, need extra practice. Make sure they do not sound breathy or unclear. You may need to adjust your embouchure slightly to make a good sound.

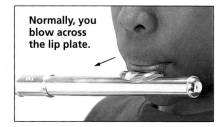

Normally, you blow across the lip plate.

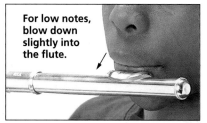

For low notes, blow down slightly into the flute.

6/8 time

Eighth beats in groups of three

In 6/8 time there are six eighth beats in a bar, arranged in two groups of three. You can count in eighth notes, or in dotted quarter notes, with two dotted quarter notes in each bar.

Dotted quarter rests

Dotted quarter rest

A dot after a rest increases its length by half, just like a dot after a note. A dotted quarter rest lasts for one and a half quarter beats.

Soeur Monique

This tune is by François Couperin (1668-1733). Couperin wrote a lot of music for the harpsichord, which was the most popular keyboard instrument before the piano was invented. This piece was originally for harpsichord and descant recorder.

A harpsichord dating from Couperin's time

The pig and the milkmaid

This tune is for a type of lively dance called a jig. Jigs come mainly from Scotland and Ireland. As you play the piece, emphasize the first and fourth eighth notes of the bar to make it sound lively.

Mezzo piano and mezzo forte

mp	*mf*
Mezzo piano	**Mezzo forte**

The signs *mp* and *mf* stand for *mezzo piano* and *mezzo forte*. In Italian, the word *mezzo* means "fairly", so *mezzo piano* means "fairly quiet" (but not as quiet as *piano*), and *mezzo forte* means "fairly loud" (but not as loud as *forte*).

Mockingbird song

Ländler

A ländler is a 17th century German folk dance. Originally it was danced outside, with lots of hopping and stamping. By the mid 18th century it was more formal and graceful, with turning and gliding movements. This new dance developed into the waltz. *Andante* means "at a walking pace", slightly slower than *moderato*.

Tempo markings

Tempo markings tell you how fast to play. They are often in Italian because music was first printed in Italy. On the right are some common tempo markings, with their meanings. There is also a complete list of all the musical words in the book on page 46.

Lento	slow
Andante	at a walking pace
Moderato	at a moderate speed
Allegretto	fairly lively, but not as fast as *allegro*
Allegro	fast and lively
Presto	very fast

Key signatures

1 sharp	**1 flat**

Sometimes there are sharp or flat signs next to the clef at the beginning of a piece. This is called the key signature. It tells you which notes to play sharp or flat throughout the piece.

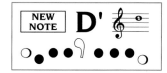

NEW NOTE **D'**

Wassail

Wassailing is a very old English custom. At Christmas and New Year, singers and musicians went from house to house, hoping to be invited to join in with the festivities. Remember to play F sharps throughout this tune.

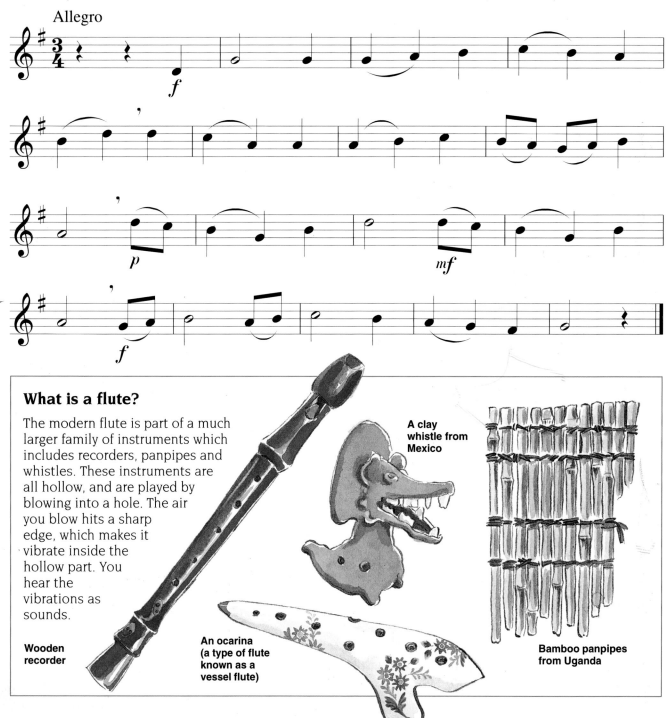

Allegro

f ' *p* *mf* *f*

What is a flute?

The modern flute is part of a much larger family of instruments which includes recorders, panpipes and whistles. These instruments are all hollow, and are played by blowing into a hole. The air you blow hits a sharp edge, which makes it vibrate inside the hollow part. You hear the vibrations as sounds.

Wooden recorder

An ocarina (a type of flute known as a vessel flute)

A clay whistle from Mexico

Bamboo panpipes from Uganda

Playing staccato

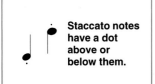

Staccato notes have a dot above or below them.

Staccato means "detached". Make the notes very short, but do not tongue too hard or they will sound breathy. Try starting each note with a "t" or "d" sound instead of "ta". In a tune, take care not to play the staccato notes louder than the other notes, and make sure they do not sound harsh.

In dulci jubilo

This German carol is probably over 700 years old. Some people say the words were first sung by angels to a man named Heinrich Suso as he sat thinking on a hill.

Sixteenth notes

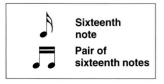

Sixteenth note

Pair of sixteenth notes

A sixteenth note lasts for half a eighth note. Groups of two, four or six sixteenth notes are often joined together.

More about breathing

When you have to take a breath between two notes, instead of during a rest, try not to interrupt the rhythm. Cut the first note a bit short and breathe quickly. Make sure the next note is not late. This can seem tricky at first, but it gets easier with practice.

Tomorrow shall be my dancing day

Incomplete bars

Four beats in a bar

First bar of tune has one beat

Last bar of tune has three beats

Sometimes the first bar of a piece is incomplete. Count the missing beats before you start to play. The last bar of the piece, or section, will also be incomplete. Together, the first and last bars make one complete bar.

Turkish march

This tune is by an Austrian composer and music publisher named Anton Diabelli (1781-1858). He once asked 50 famous composers in Vienna to write a variation on one of his waltzes.

Vienna

Moderato

Dynamics in brackets

mf (p)	Second
mp (mf)	dynamic in brackets

Repeated sections often have two sets of dynamics. Follow the dynamics without brackets the first time, then the ones in brackets when you repeat.

Czech polka

This tune is by Johann Strauss II. The polka became popular in ballrooms throughout Europe during the 19th century. It is a very lively, energetic dance. Follow the dynamics carefully in this piece.

Dancing a polka

Allegretto

Eighth rests

An eighth rest lasts for half a quarter note.

More dynamics

pp **Pianissimo**

ff **Fortissimo**

In Italian, *-issimo* on the end of a word means "very". P*ianissimo*, written *pp*, means "very quiet" and *fortissimo*, written *ff*, means "very loud". When you play very loudly, keep your tongue low in your mouth so the notes sound properly.

El *vito*

This tune is a song from an area of southern Spain called Andalusia. Play it with a strong beat, and watch out for the tricky rhythms.

Early flutes

Flutes have been played all around the world since the earliest times. They were probably made by accident at first, from pieces of bamboo or hollow bones. Then people realized they could play different notes by altering the length of the tube, or covering and uncovering holes in it.

Bone recorders which may be up to 16,000 years old have been found in caves in France. Pipes were played several thousand years ago in Egypt, India and China. The first flutes to be held sideways (called transverse flutes) were probably used over 2,800 years ago.

Egyptian paintings, dating from around 4,000 years ago, often show people playing pipes.

Some Greek paintings from around 2,500 years ago show flute players. Many flutes had two pipes, both with finger holes.

These Chinese flute players were painted over 1,000 years ago. They are playing a mixture of vertical and transverse flutes.

Sumer is icumen in

This 13th century song is a type of piece called a canon. In a canon, several people sing or play the same tune, starting a few bars after each other. This piece is the earliest known canon. Watch out for the sharps in the key signature.

You could play this tune with some friends. When the first player reaches the number 2, the second player starts at the beginning. When the first player reaches the number 3, the third player starts, and so on. Play at a steady speed, and do not stop if you go wrong. You could record yourself playing the tune on your own, then play the tape and join in with it.

Manuscript of the opening bars of *Sumer is icumen in*

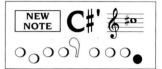

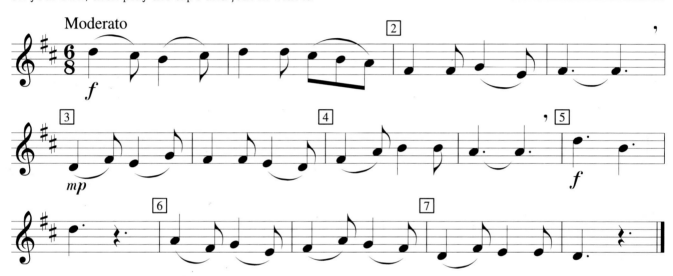

2/4 time

This time signature means there are two quarter beats in every bar.

Naturals

A natural sign cancels a sharp or flat earlier in the bar or in the key signature.

Hoedown

A hoedown is a lively 19th century American dance. Tap a foot or click your flute keys shut in the rests.

22

Lullaby

This tune is by Johannes Brahms (1833-1897), a German composer and pianist. Brahms came from a poor family in Hamburg, and as a teenager helped to support his family by playing in cafés. He was fascinated by music from around the world and wrote some famous arrangements of Hungarian dances. *Cantabile* means "in a singing style" and *legato* means "smoothly".

Hamburg, where Brahms was born

Common time

	4 quarter beats in a bar

This time signature means the same as 4/4 (four quarter beats in a bar). It is called common time.

Now is the month of maying

This tune by the English composer Thomas Morley (1557-1602) is from a madrigal. A madrigal is a song for several voices, often about love or nature. Morley wrote many songs, and also one of the first important books on music, called A *Plaine and Easie Introduction to Practicall Musicke*. This gave advice on how to compose music and perform it.

Singers performing a madrigal

Playing G sharp

To play G sharp, you position your fingers as though you were playing G, then press an extra key. This is the thin, curved key which sticks out just next to your left-hand third finger. Press it with your left-hand little finger.

NEW NOTE · G♯

Serenade

This tune is by Joseph Haydn (1732-1809), an Austrian composer. He wrote a great deal of music, including 100 pieces for orchestra (called symphonies). Many of these had nicknames, for example "The Hen", "The Clock", "The Surprise", "The Schoolmaster" and "The Bear".

Originally a serenade was a love song sung in the evening.

Lazy day blues

Blues music began in America at the end of the 19th century. It developed from songs which people sang while they worked. This tune contains lots of dotted eighth notes. A dot after an eighth note makes it last for one and a half eighth beats. Try clapping this piece before you play it, making the rhythm sound slightly more relaxed than usual.

D.C. al Fine

D.C. al Fine

Fine

The instruction D.C. *al Fine* at the end of a piece stands for *Da Capo al Fine*. This tells you to go back to the beginning of the piece and start playing the music again. When you reach the *Fine* sign, you stop.

Sharps and flats

Below is a new note called E flat. It has the same fingering as D sharp. This is because E flat and D sharp are two names for the same note, between D and E. If the key signature has sharps, this note is called D sharp. If the key signature has flats, it is called E flat. Other notes with two names are B flat or A sharp, D flat or C sharp, and A flat or G sharp.

Old French tune

This tune is by a composer called Pyotr Il'yich Tchaikovsky (1840-1893). Tchaikovsky wrote several ballets, including *The Sleeping Beauty*, *Swan Lake* and *The Nutcracker*. After the D.C. *al Fine*, only play the first section once. The key signature tells you to play B flats and E flats.

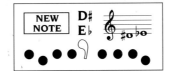

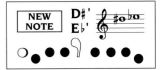

Sarabande

A sarabande was originally a 16th century Spanish dance. Since then, many slow, stately dances with three beats in a bar have been called sarabandes. Often they begin with the rhythm used at the start of this tune.

Dancing a sarabande

Playing high notes

Most high notes on the flute have the same fingering as the lower version of the same note. For example, high E (E') has the same fingering as ordinary E. To play the higher note you tighten your lips a bit, blow a little harder, and aim the air upward slightly. Try playing some high versions of the notes you already know. Keep your face and body relaxed, and try to make a good sound which is not harsh or breathy.

Do not blow down into the flute, as you did for playing low notes.

Make sure your top lip is firm.

Tighten your lips a bit, but keep your cheek muscles relaxed.

Cover slightly more of the blow hole than usual.

Move your jaw forward a bit.

Remember not to grip your flute too tightly.

Always breathe deeply and blow from the diaphragm.

Getting louder and quieter

These signs are a type of dynamic marking. The sign that gets wider on the right tells you to get gradually louder. The sign that is wider on the left tells you to get gradually quieter.

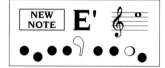

La *bourbonnaise*

This is another piece by Couperin. Play it through once, then practice any tricky bars separately. Also practice making a contrast between the different dynamics. Don't play the *mezzo forte* or *forte* sections too loudly or you will not be able to get louder at the end of the tune.

Couperin

Burlesque

A burlesque is a type of light-hearted piece popular in the early 1700s. This one is by Leopold Mozart (1719-1787), father of the famous composer Wolfgang Amadeus Mozart. It is from a collection of music which Leopold wrote for his daughter.

Leopold Mozart (left) with his son Wolfgang and daughter Nannerl

First-time and second-time bars

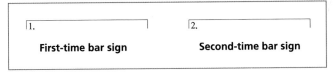

First-time bar sign   **Second-time bar sign**

Some tunes with repeats have two different endings. The first time you play the music, you play the first-time bar, then repeat the section. The second time, you play the second-time bar instead.

In the meadow

This is a type of Austrian folk song. In it, the singer quickly alternates between high and low notes. This is known as yodeling.

A singer yodeling

Gavotte

A gavotte is a lively country dance from the Pays de Gap region of France. In the 17th and 18th centuries, it also became popular as a court dance. This gavotte is by an English composer named Samuel Arnold (1740-1802).

The gavotte developed from this stately, swaying dance, called a branle ("brawl").

Minuet

This tune is by Henry Purcell (1659-1695), an English composer and court musician. During his career he worked for three kings: Charles II, James II and William III. *Ritardando*, often abbreviated to *rit.*, means "get gradually slower".

Charles II's palace, where Purcell worked

Crescendo and *diminuendo*

cresc.
dim.

Cresc. (short for *crescendo*) means "get gradually louder". *Dim.* (or *diminuendo*) means "get gradually quieter".

Polish dance

This tune is a type of quick dance called a mazurka. The dancers tap their heels in time with the music, usually on the second or third beat of each bar.

A 19th century ballroom version of a mazurka

Accents

♩ >

An accent above or below a note tells you to play it more forcefully than usual.

Playing A sharp

A sharp is another name for B flat (see page 25). Play it with the fingering you use for B flat.

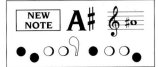

The Ardelean woman

29

Pause marks

The next tune contains a sign called a pause mark. It tells you to make the note last for a bit longer.

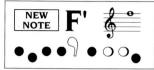
NEW NOTE **F'**

A *virgin most pure*

This tune is a traditional English carol. Try to play it very expressively, emphasizing the changes in dynamics and speed. The words *a tempo* tell you to return to your original speed after you have slowed down during the *ritardando*.

In the 12th century, a carol was a dance and a song combined.

German dance

This tune is by a composer named Franz Schubert (1797-1828). He wrote many pieces, including over 600 songs. Although he gave only one public concert, his music is still very popular today.

Schubert had his music performed at parties for his friends.

Hot chicken strut

There are lots of unusual rhythms in this tune. Clap it through slowly at first, tapping a foot in the rests so you do not leave them out. Make the music sound very rhythmic and lively. Watch out for the notes with accents.

The development of the flute

Until the 17th century, flutes had six finger holes but no keys. They were hard to play quickly and in tune.

In the late 1600s, instrument makers began to design flutes with a key for the right-hand little finger. This added an extra note, improved the tuning, and made flutes more popular. The first book on flute playing was written in 1707.

By the late 1700s flutes were frequently used in orchestras. Many were designed with four, six or even eight keys, but these often fell off. The tuning was better, but still not perfect.

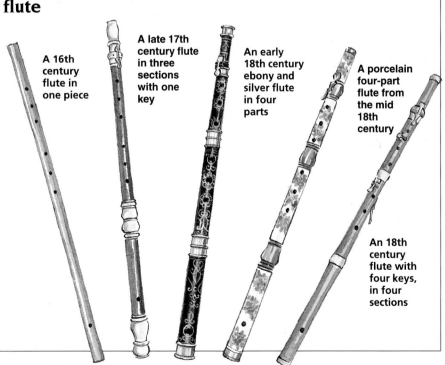

A 16th century flute in one piece

A late 17th century flute in three sections with one key

An early 18th century ebony and silver flute in four parts

A porcelain four-part flute from the mid 18th century

An 18th century flute with four keys, in four sections

Grace notes

A grace note is played very quickly just before a beat to decorate the next note. It is written as a very small eighth note with a diagonal line through the stem.

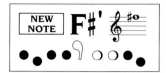

Romance

This tune is from a piano piece by Beethoven. As a young man, Beethoven was a very successful pianist, and wrote a lot of music which he performed himself at concerts.

Beethoven composing at his piano

Boehm's flute

A German flute player, Theobald Boehm (1794-1881), made the first flutes which were perfectly in tune. These had 12 holes, spaced in a certain way, which the player operated using a system of keys, rods and levers. Boehm's flutes were louder and easier to play than earlier ones, and soon became very popular. One of them is the standard model used today.

Two of Boehm's flutes

Basse danse

The basse danse is a graceful, gliding dance from the 15th and 16th centuries. This music for the dance appears (along with the *Air des bouffons* tune on page 8) in the earliest known book of dance steps and music, *Orchésographie*. This was published in 1558 by a French writer named Thoinot Arbeau (1520-1595).

Long pointed shoes meant dancers had to tread carefully.

Mazurka

This tune is from a ballet called *Coppélia* by a French composer, Léo Delibes (1836-1891). The ballet tells the story of a young man named Franz who falls in love with a beautiful life-sized doll named Coppélia. Swanhilda, the woman Franz was about to marry, plays a trick by pretending to be Coppélia come alive. Eventually, Franz realizes Coppélia is only a doll and marries Swanhilda.

A scene from *Coppélia* showing Franz and Swanhilda dancing together

Gavotte

This tune is by Purcell. Purcell began writing simple songs and keyboard music when he was very young. His first piece was published when he was only eight years old. The word *leggiero* means "light". Play almost staccato, so the music feels like a dance.

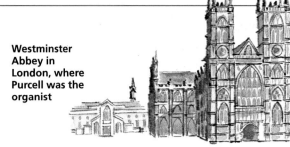

Westminster Abbey in London, where Purcell was the organist

Boy's chorus

This tune by the French composer Georges Bizet (1838-1875) is from an opera (play set to music) called *Carmen*. *Carmen* was not a success at the first performance, but today it is one of the most popular operas ever written.

Bizet

Greensleeves

This tune became very popular in the 16th century, and has remained popular ever since. At this time, ordinary people thought music was a very important part of their education, and often sang and played instruments with their friends.

A singer accompanied by a flute player and a woman playing a stringed instrument called a lute

Modern flutes

The concert flute is the most common type of flute. The piccolo is half the size of this and plays an octave higher. Alto and bass flutes play lower notes. The bass flute is the lowest, playing an octave below a concert flute. Most flutes today are made from nickel, silver, gold or platinum.

Gold and platinum flutes are very expensive though. Some flute players who play a lot of early music, dating from before metal flutes were invented, use special wooden flutes like the ones used when the music was written.

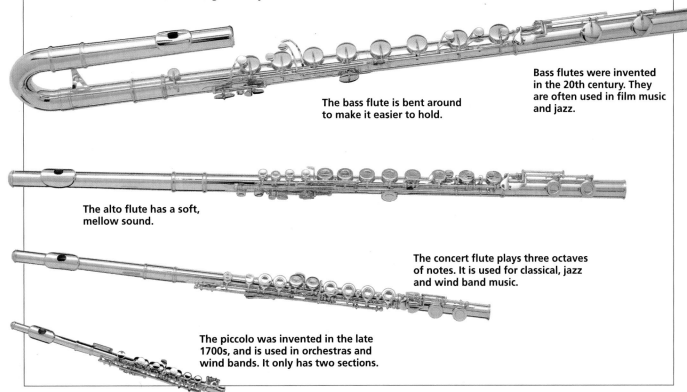

Bass flutes were invented in the 20th century. They are often used in film music and jazz.

The bass flute is bent around to make it easier to hold.

The alto flute has a soft, mellow sound.

The concert flute plays three octaves of notes. It is used for classical, jazz and wind band music.

The piccolo was invented in the late 1700s, and is used in orchestras and wind bands. It only has two sections.

Galop

This dance tune is by Offenbach. It is from an operetta called *Orpheus in the Underworld*. A galop was a fast and lively ballroom dance from Germany which was popular throughout Europe in the 19th century.

Scenes from before, during and after a galop

Can-can

This tune is also from *Orpheus in the Underworld*. It comes immediately after the galop tune above. When you have practiced both of them, you could try playing them straight through, one after the other, to hear how they sound in the operetta.

The can-can involves a lot of high-kicking.

36

Hornpipe

A hornpipe is an energetic British dance popular from the 16th century to the 19th century. *Accelerando* (shortened to *accel.*) means "get gradually faster".

Sailors dancing a hornpipe

Practice tips

✔ Play low G then high G' several times making sure you hit the high note cleanly each time.

✔ Practice taking slow, deep breaths, keeping your body completely relaxed.

✔ Record your playing on a cassette and listen to it. This can help you spot mistakes you might not have noticed before, and remind you to play expressively. Dynamics might not be as clear to listeners as they are to you when you are playing.

Tarantella

A tarantella is an Italian dance which gradually gets faster and faster. This tune is divided into five sections. Parts A, C and E are identical. Learn one section at a time, then play the whole piece at a steady speed. When you can do this, try getting faster as you play.

Dancing a tarantella

Memorizing music

When you can play a tune well, try it without the music. Only look at the music if you get stuck.

Then put the music away and start again. You will soon be able to play it all from memory.

Polonaise

This tune is by the German composer and organist Johann Sebastian Bach (1685-1750). A polonaise is a stately dance from Poland. This one is from a set of keyboard pieces which Bach wrote for his wife, Anna Magdalena.

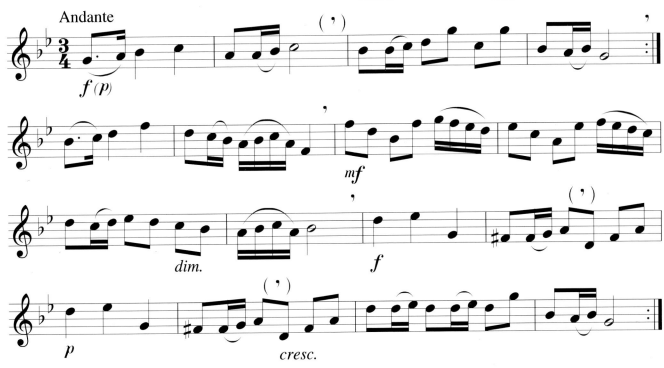

Flutes from around the world

Today there are many different types of flutes played around the world. You can see some of them below.

This Japanese flute is made from a piece of bamboo.

The wooden flute below has two pipes. It is played in parts of Central Europe.

This flute is from Polynesia. The player blows into it through one nostril.

This large wooden flute comes from Slovakia.

The South African flute below is made from a hollow fruit shell and a piece of cane. The player blows across a hole in the shell. There are finger holes in the cane.

This flute from Peru is called a whistling pot. It is partly filled with water, then blown to make a whistling sound.

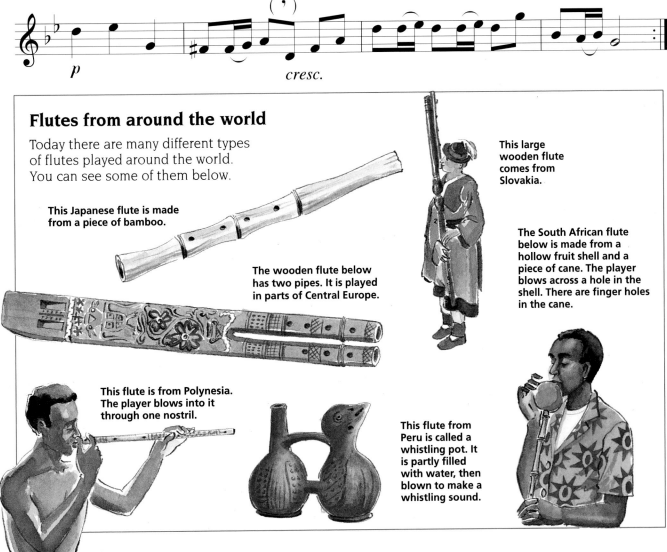

Intermezzo

An intermezzo was originally a piece of music played between the scenes of a play or opera. This intermezzo, by the German composer Felix Mendelssohn (1809-1847), was written to go with a play called A *Midsummer Night's Dream* by William Shakespeare. Mendelssohn conducted several orchestras and choirs, and organized concerts and music festivals. He also founded a special music school in Leipzig, in Germany.

Mendelssohn

Early one morning

40

Playing duets

Duets are pieces for two people. Each person plays a different part. The tunes below are duet parts to play with the tunes on the opposite page. Before you play with someone, learn your own parts carefully. Check your flutes are in tune with each other by playing an A together. You can make a flute sound lower by pulling the head joint out a bit from the body. Then decide how fast to play and count a bar out loud before you start.

Intermezzo (Duet part)

Early one morning (Duet part)

Thistledown waltz

You can play the top line of this piece on your own,
or with a piano to accompany you (make sure your
flute is in tune with the piano). It should sound very
smooth and light. Remember, D flat is another name
for C sharp, and A flat is another name for G sharp.
Rallentando (or *rall.*) means "get gradually slower".

Andante grazioso

This piece is by Wolfgang Amadeus Mozart (1756-1791). Mozart started to write his own music when he was only five years old. The word *grazioso* means "graceful". The picture on the right shows the Augarten concert hall in Vienna, where Mozart's music was often performed.

Andante grazioso

p cantabile

pp

mf

mp

p

pp

First class stomp

A stomp is an energetic dance. The music is in a style known as jazz. Try clapping the rhythm before you start to play. Watch out for the dotted eighth rest in bar seven. The music should sound relaxed and unhurried, but with a strong, steady beat. If you play this piece with a piano, count carefully and listen to how the rhythms fit together.

Dancing to a jazz band

44

Music help

This list explains the Italian words used in this book. Each Italian word has its pronunciation after it (in **bold** letters). Read these pronunciation letters as if they were English words.

accelerando	**a-chel-er-an-doh**	getting faster
andante	**an-dan-tay**	at a walking pace, a bit slower than moderato
allegretto	**a-luh-gretto**	fairly lively, not as fast as allegro
allegro	**a-leg-ro**	fast and lively
a tempo	**ah tempo**	at the original speed
cantabile	**cant-ah-be-lay**	in a singing style
crescendo (cresc.)	**cruh-shen-doh**	getting louder
D.C. *al Fine*	**dee cee al fee-nay**	repeat from the beginning to the Fine sign
diminuendo (dim.)	**dim-in-you-en-doh**	getting quieter
Fine	**fee-nay**	stop
forte (f)	**for-tay**	loud
fortissimo (ff)	**for-tiss-im-oh**	very loud
grazioso	**grat-see-oh-so**	gracefully
legato	**leg-ah-toe**	smoothly
leggiero	**led-jee-air-oh**	lightly
lento	**len-toe**	slow
mezzo forte (mf)	**met-so for-tay**	fairly loud
mezzo piano (mp)	**met-so pee-ah-no**	fairly quiet
moderato	**mod-er-ah-toe**	at a moderate speed
pianissimo (pp)	**pee-an-iss-im-oh**	very quiet
piano (p)	**pee-ah-no**	quiet
presto	**press-toe**	very fast
rallentando (rall.)	**rall-en-tan-doh**	getting slower
ritardando (rit.)	**rit-ar-dan-doh**	getting slower
staccato	**stack-ah-toe**	detached, short

Fingering chart

This chart shows the fingering for all the notes in this book. The fingering diagrams are explained on page 3.

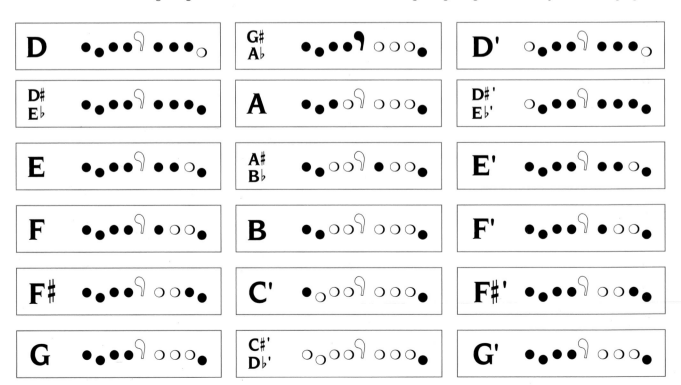

Flute music to listen to

Below are some suggestions for flute music you could try listening to.

Arnold	Concerto no.1	**Godard**	Suite de Trois Morceaux
	Concerto no.2	**Gossec**	Tambourin
J. S. Bach	Sonatas	**Handel**	Sonatas
	Suite no.2 in B minor	**Haydn**	Sonatas
R. R. Bennett	Sonatina for solo flute	**Hindemith**	Sonata
Berkeley	Sonata	**Ibert**	Concerto
	Sonatina	**Martinu**	First sonata
Boismortier	Sonatas	**Messaien**	Le merle noir
	Concertos	**Mozart**	Andante in C
Bozza	Agreotide		Concertos
Chaminade	Concertino		Concerto for flute and harp
Debussy	Syrinx	**Nielsen**	Concerto
Doppler	Fantaisie Pastorale	**Poulenc**	Sonata
	Hongroise	**Prokofiev**	Sonata no.2
Fauré	Fantaisie	**Quantz**	Concerts
	Pavane	**Roussel**	Jouers de la flûte
	Sicilienne		Andante et Scherzo
Frederick the		**Telemann**	Sonatas
Great	Sonatas		Concertos
	Concertos	**Varèse**	Density 21.5
Gluck	Dance of the Blessed Spirits	**Vivaldi**	Concertos
	(from *Orpheus in the Underworld*)	**Weber**	Sonata

Index

Acknowledgements

The publishers would like to thank Jessica Bailey, Ricardo Bynoe and Ben Chudleigh who were photographed for this book; also Bill Lewington Musical Instruments, London, for supplying the flutes in the photographs.